TIMELINES OF
AMERICAN HISTORY ™

A Timeline of the Constitutional Convention

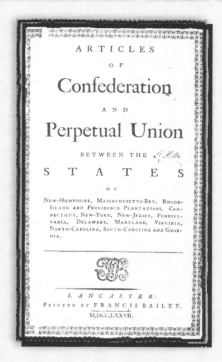

ARTICLES

OF

Confederation

AND

Perpetual Union

BETWEEN THE

STATES

OF

NEW-HAMPSHIRE, MASSACHUSETTS-BAY, RHODE-
ISLAND AND PROVIDENCE PLANTATIONS, CON-
NECTICUT, NEW-YORK, NEW-JERSEY, PENNSYL-
VANIA, DELAWARE, MARYLAND, VIRGINIA,
NORTH-CAROLINA, SOUTH-CAROLINA AND GEOR-
GIA.

LANCASTER:
PRINTED BY FRANCIS BAILEY.
M,DCC,LXXVII.

Sandra Giddens and Owen Giddens

rosen central ™

The Rosen Publishing Group, Inc., New York

Published in 2004 by The Rosen Publishing Group, Inc.
29 East 21st Street, New York, NY 10010

Library of Congress Cataloging-in-Publication Data

Giddens, Sandra.
A timeline of the Constitutional Convention / Sandra Giddens and Owen
Giddens. —1st ed. p. cm. — (Timelines of American history)
Includes bibliographical references and index.
Contents: In the beginning — The Articles of Confederation —A meeting of minds —
The Constitution is approved.
ISBN 0-8239-4535-9 (library binding)
1. United States—Politics and government—1783-1789—Chronology—Juvenile litera-
ture. 2. United States. Constitutional Convention (1787)—Juvenile literature. 3. Constitutional
history—United States—Chronology—Juvenile literature. 4. United States—Politics and
government—To 1775—Chronology—Juvenile literature. 5. United States—Politics
and government—1775-1783—Chronology—Juvenile literature. [1. United States.
Constitutional Convention (1787) 2. United States—Politics and government—To
1775—Chronology. 3. United States—Politics and government—1775-1783—
Chronology. 4. United States—Politics and government—1783-1789—Chronology.] I.
Giddens, Owen. II. Title. III. Series.
E303.G53 2003
342.7302'92—dc22

2003016863

Manufactured in the United States of America

On the cover: George Washington presides over the Second Constitutional Convention in
1787 in this undated painting by Howard Chandler Christie.
On the title page: The title page of the U.S. Articles of Confederation, created in 1777 in
Williamsburg, Virginia.

Contents

1

In the Beginning

I n the steaming hot summer of 1787, the Constitution of the United States was written. A group of about 200 men gathered in Philadelphia to discuss their ideas about the United States and its future. The U.S. Constitution remains among the most enduring constitutions in the world. Its direct origins probably trace back to Great Britain, where, in 1215, British nobility wanted laws drafted to protect them. At that time, the British forced King John to agree to the Magna Carta. The Pilgrims, who later came to America, used their knowledge of British law to govern the new country.

Pilgrims aboard the *Mayflower* watch Myles Standish sign the Mayflower Compact. The 1620 document outlined the government of the Plymouth Colony and established its first governor, William Bradford.

1215

The Magna Carta, or Great Charter, guarantees that the British king will not take lands from nobility or collect taxes from them without their consent. Trials are decided by a group of jurors. Over the centuries, these rights were extended to all people.

Settlers in this painting arrive on the shores of Virginia in 1607 to a colony they name Jamestown. Drought and disease will kill most of them within eight months.

1607

The first permanent English colony is founded at Jamestown, Virginia.

1620

Pilgrims, a group of religious outcasts, set sail from Great Britain for the New World (America). Before landing, the Pilgrims develop the Mayflower Compact, which contains information about how they would govern the new land.

Taxation Without Representation

By 1733, there were thirteen colonies, and by 1775, there were more than one million colonists. The British king and Parliament had legal authority over the colonies and imposed taxes on the colonists. The colonists believed that Great Britain did not have the right to tax them without their representation in Parliament. They felt there should be "no taxation without representation." In Massachusetts, people called out against taxation and suggested some form of united protest throughout the colonies.

Massachusetts governor Thomas Hutchinson flees rioters in 1765 after the British imposed the Stamp Act on colonists. Hutchinson was a British loyalist who believed the Stamp Act was justified. His refusal to return British cargo ships after colonists refused to pay the taxes on British imports led to the Boston Tea Party in 1773.

1764

Sugar Act: Great Britain desires revenue from its North American colonies and increases duties on non-British goods shipped to the colonies.

Currency Act: Great Britain prohibits American colonies from issuing their own currency, an act that angers American colonists.

1765

Quartering Act: In a move that further angers colonists, the Quartering Act requires the colonies to provide barracks and supplies to British troops.

In 1773, Boston colonists disguised as Native Americans emptied crates of tea from British merchant ships into Boston Harbor in the event known as the Boston Tea Party.

Stamp Act: The British Parliament's first direct tax on the colonies is established. Patrick Henry makes a speech against the Stamp Act to Virginia leaders.

1773

Tea Act: Americans boycott British tea.

Boston Tea Party: A group of colonists dress as Native Americans and dump tea from British ships into Boston Harbor.

7

The Revolutionary War

Soon the colonists' protests led to the Revolutionary War. Both the colonists and the British believed in their cause. The British felt that the thirteen colonies belonged to them. Although the colonies were officially British, the nearly 200 years spent away from the king made them seem independent. The colonists no longer wanted to be under the thumb of the British monarchy. Although the colonists lost many battles, they held off the British with the assistance of French troops. The last battle took place in Yorktown, Virginia, in 1871. At that time, colonial and French soldiers captured 8,000 British soldiers.

British troops open fire upon colonial minutemen in 1775 at the Battle of Lexington, beginning the American Revolutionary War.

1774

Twelve of the thirteen colonies send representatives to the First Continental Congress in Philadelphia. Colonists avoid using British goods, and committees are formed to enforce the ban.

1775

Colonial soldiers fight British soldiers at Lexington and Concord, Massachusetts, beginning the Revolutionary War.

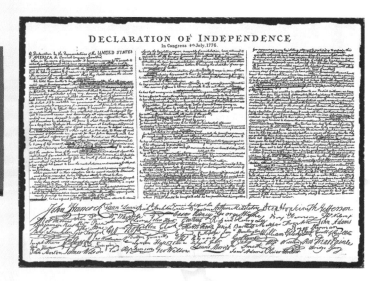

This is the final version of the Declaration of Independence, which had been previously adopted on July 4, 1776, by fifty-six members of Congress.

1776

Members of the Second Continental Congress write and approve the Declaration of Independence. American colonists declare their independence from Great Britain.

1777

On June 14, Congress approves the flag of the United States. The design contains thirteen alternating red and white stripes and a blue field with thirteen white stars.

1778

France joins the Revolutionary War and sends soldiers to assist the colonies.

1781

American forces led by General George Washington are victorious in a surprise attack against the British at the Battle of Yorktown.

Betsy Ross Flag 1777

This print commemorates the design of the first American flag, which was sewn by Betsy Ross and adopted by Congress in 1777.

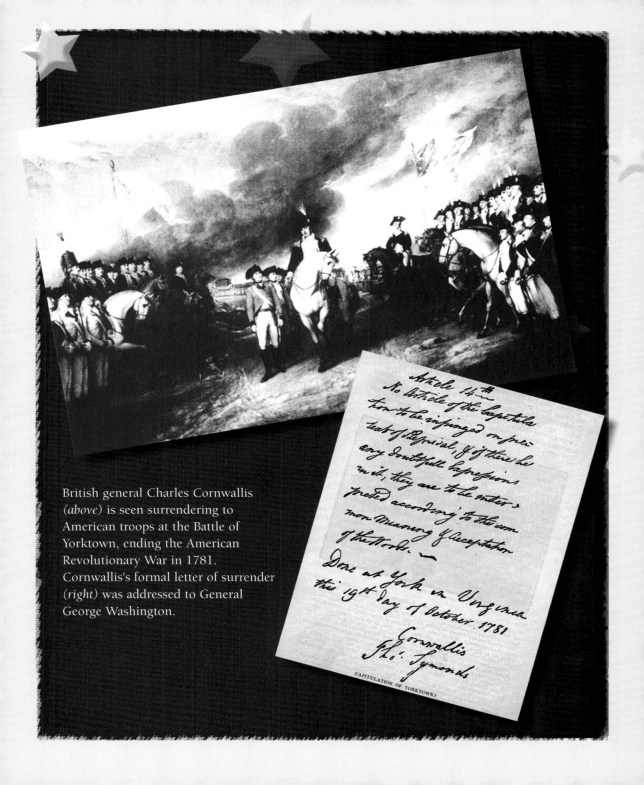

British general Charles Cornwallis (*above*) is seen surrendering to American troops at the Battle of Yorktown, ending the American Revolutionary War in 1781. Cornwallis's formal letter of surrender (*right*) was addressed to General George Washington.

2

The Articles of Confederation

I n 1783, Great Britain and America signed the Treaty of Paris. The colonists finally won the war and their independence. The thirteen colonies had before been separate political states with their own governments, but they had joined together for the cause of independence. Now known as the United States, the country needed a new central government. The term "United States" refers to an association or confederation. A system of rules called the Articles of Confederation established the first national U.S. government. These guidelines gave Congress some control, but each state had more power over itself than the central government had over it.

The Treaty of Paris was an agreement between Great Britain and America that formally ended the Revolutionary War. The treaty recognized the United States as an independent country.

⭐ 1781

The Articles of Confederation establishes the first national U.S. government and gives Congress control over foreign affairs, defense, the postal system, and Indian affairs. The states approve the Articles of Confederation.

⭐ 1782

British and colonial leaders meet in Paris, France, to begin peace talks. They write the Treaty of Paris.

⭐ 1783

The American Revolution ends. Congress approves the Treaty of Paris. The colonies become fully independent from Great Britain.

On November 15, 1777, the Continental Congress adopted the Articles of Confederation *(top)*, which served as the first constitution of the United States until 1789. This British map *(below)*, created in 1784, illustrates the original thirteen colonies of America.

State Vs. Federal Power

Americans feared that individual state governments could cause the states to drift apart. By 1785, James Madison and other statesmen knew that the Articles of Confederation had to be rewritten. The states were not united. Small rebellions by the individual states to overpower the national government alerted statesmen that the system was troubled.

Early in 1786, at the Virginia General Assembly, Madison proposed a convention to review the Articles of Confederation that autumn. Madison took a year to study and learn about past attempts to create republics and confederacies. He wanted to help America form a stronger union.

Gilbert Stuart painted this portrait of James Madison, the fourth U.S. president, who is remembered as the father of the Constitution.

Thomas Sully captured a likeness of Thomas Jefferson, the third president of the United States, in this nineteenth-century portrait.

The capitol of colonial America, shown in this contemporary photograph, was built in Williamsburg, Virginia, in 1705. It served as the meeting place of the Virginia General Assembly.

1784 ★

Thomas Jefferson proposes a plan for dividing the western territories and providing a temporary government for the west. New York City is the temporary capital of the United States.

1786 ★

The Virginia legislature passes Jefferson's Ordinance of Religious Freedom. It guarantees that no person should be discriminated against because of his or her religious beliefs. This statute would later serve as the model for the First Amendment of the United States Constitution.

3

A Meeting of Minds

A mid calls for a stronger central government, Congress recommended a resolution calling for a Constitutional Convention. It was time for representatives of the thirteen states to come together. The delegates traveled treacherous roads by horseback and coach in order to reach Philadelphia. The first meeting of the Constitutional Convention was held on May 25, 1787. The delegates included lawyers and bankers, mostly from wealthy and conservative ranks of society. Farmers and merchants were also represented. Jonathan Dayton, at age twenty-six, was the youngest state representative, and eighty-one-year-old Benjamin Franklin was the eldest. George

Karl Bodmer created this engraving of the Pennsylvania State House (Independence Hall) in Philadelphia, the meeting place of the Constitutional Convention in 1787.

Washington presided over the meeting. Records show that fifty-five delegates attended, but only thirty-nine people actually signed the Constitution.

★ **January 25, 1787**
Shays's Rebellion: About 1,500 farmers led by Daniel Shays attempt a raid on a government arsenal in Springfield, Massachusetts. General Benjamin Lincoln arrives with reinforcements from Boston to pursue the rebels.

★ **May 25, 1787**
The Constitutional Convention begins in the Pennsylvania State House (Independence Hall) in Philadelphia.

The blacksmith in this woodcut expresses his anger over rising taxes enforced by the United States to help pay off war debts. These high taxes forced many merchants out of business. Their rebellious response, led by Daniel Shays, took place in 1787.

17

Determining the Role of Government

Every state but Rhode Island sent representatives to the convention. The delegates had to examine government policies. State representatives considered if there should be a king to oversee the government or if states could instead govern themselves. When the delegates began debating, it soon became clear that a new government was needed. Among the main points of discussion were state and national limits of power, the number of representatives in Congress for each state, and how those representatives should be elected.

George Washington captures the attention of delegates in this engraving depicting the debate inside Independence Hall at the Constitutional Convention in Philadelphia in 1787.

June 19, 1787

Delegates from each of the thirteen states (except Rhode Island) vote to create an entirely new form of national government. This new government is separated into three branches: legislative, executive, and judiciary.

September 17, 1787

Thirty-nine delegates approve and sign the final draft of the new Constitution.

September 19, 1787

The new Constitution is made public. Printed copies of the text are distributed. A storm of controversy arises. People expect a revision of the Articles of Confederation, not a new central government with similarities to the British system they had just overthrown.

This is the original signed Constitution of the United States, drafted in secret by delegates in Philadelphia during the summer of 1787 during the Constitutional Convention.

September 28, 1787

Congress votes to send the Constitution to the state legislatures for approval. In order to pass, it requires a majority agreement of nine states.

FEDERALIST:

A COLLECTION

OF *C. W. Har*

ESSAYS,

WRITTEN IN FAVOUR OF THE

NEW CONSTITUTION,

AS AGREED UPON BY THE FEDERAL CONVENTION,
SEPTEMBER 17, 1787.

IN TWO VOLUMES.

VOL. I.

This is the title page of the Federalist Papers, a series of essays published in newspapers in 1787 and 1788 by James Madison, Alexander Hamilton, and John Jay in order to help promote the ratification of the U.S. Constitution.

4

The Constitution Is Approved

On September 17, 1787, the Constitution was signed and sent to Congress. Public debate over its contents had begun. Although it specified that only nine states were needed to approve the new government, everyone hoped it would be universally accepted. Printed copies of the Constitution were forwarded to each of the thirteen state legislatures for acceptance. Between 1787 and 1788, Alexander Hamilton, James Madison, and John Jay wrote eighty-five essays in an attempt to explain and defend the new laws. Some statesmen opposed the new Constitution. Many people joined in the debate by giving speeches, and writing articles, pamphlets, and letters.

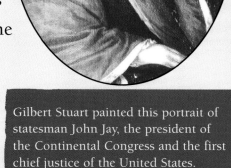

Gilbert Stuart painted this portrait of statesman John Jay, the president of the Continental Congress and the first chief justice of the United States.

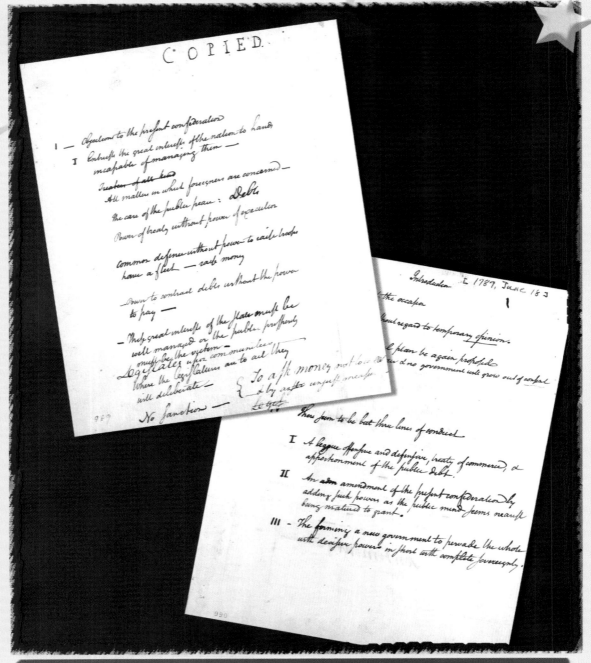

The notes on this page are written in the hand of Alexander Hamilton in preparation for a speech about his philosophy of government made to delegates at the Constitutional Convention on June 18, 1787.

★ **October 27, 1787**
Federalists believe in a strong, centralized government. They approve of the new Constitution and begin publishing essays in favor of its approval.

★ **December 7, 1787**
Delaware is the first of nine states to approve the Constitution.

★ **June 21, 1788**
The Constitution is approved, or ratified, by nine states.

This portrait of Alexander Hamilton is a detail of a mural by Constantino Brumidi. The mural is located inside the U.S. Capitol in Washington, D.C.

★ **July 2, 1788**
Congress announces that the Constitution has been adopted.

★ **October 10, 1788**
Congress grants ten square miles (twenty-six square kilometers) of land to the national government to establish a federal capital.

Adopting the Constitution

By June 21, 1788, conventions in nine states had decided to vote in favor of the new government. New Hampshire became the ninth state to ratify the new Constitution, making its adoption official. Preceding New Hampshire were Delaware, Pennsylvania, New

The Thirteen States with Dates of Ratification

1787

December 7	Delaware
December 12	Pennsylvania
December 18	New Jersey

1788

January 2	Georgia
January 9	Connecticut
February 6	Massachusetts
April 28	Maryland
May 23	South Carolina
June 21	New Hampshire
June 25	Virginia
July 26	New York

1789

November 21	North Carolina

1790

May 26	Rhode Island

This undated woodcut, *The Blessings of the Constitution*, marks the creation of the laws that govern the United States.

This illustration shows the *Hamilton* passing the fort of Bowling Green in New York City, where members of Congress celebrated the ratification of the U.S. Constitution.

Jersey, Georgia, Connecticut, Massachusetts, Maryland, and South Carolina. Virginia and New York ratified shortly after New Hampshire, followed by North Carolina in November 1789. Rhode Island did not join the union until 1790.

There was never any question as to who should be the first president of the United States. In fact, the electors of every state voted for George Washington. He traveled to New York City, and on April 30, 1789, President George Washington delivered the first inaugural address. Washington adopted the first ten amendments, which are known as

25

George Washington takes an oath of office in this undated engraving. Washington was inaugurated as the first president of the United States on April 30, 1789, in a joint session of Congress in Federal Hall in New York City.

the Bill of Rights. These established the fundamental rights of American citizens such as the freedoms of speech, religion, and the press. The Bill of Rights also protected people against unreasonable searches of their homes and provided a fair and speedy trial by jury.

★ 1789
North Carolina joins the union. The federal government begins functioning. George Washington becomes the first president of the United States. Members of Congress are elected by the states. New York City is made the capital of the United States.

★ 1790
Rhode Island joins the union. The United States capital is moved to Philadelphia.

★ 1791
The Bill of Rights is approved and added to the Constitution. George Washington chooses a permanent site for the new U.S. capital. It is named Washington, D.C., in his honor.

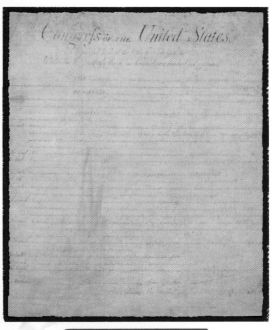

The U. S. Bill of Rights

Timelines Show Cause and Effect

Timelines are helpful tools that may be used by students to see the progress of history over a defined period. The laws governing the United States were decided over time. For instance, when reviewing the timelines in this book, we can see the exact amount of time that spanned between events that inspired the Constitution and the time in which it was ratified. Timelines can be useful to students in other ways, too. Sometimes, just glancing at timelines can help us learn about the causes and effects of certain situations. By looking at the timelines in this book, for example, we can learn that because the states challenged the national government, statesmen were alerted that the national system required their review.

Glossary

amendment (uh-MEND-ment)   An addition or a change to the Constitution.

Articles of Confederation (AR-tih-kulz UV kun-feh-deh-RAY-shun) The laws that governed the United States before the Constitution was created.

barracks (BAR-iks)   The building where soldiers live.

boycott (BOY-kaht)   To join with others in refusing to buy from or deal with a person, nation, or business; a refusal to support something.

Congress (KON-gres)   The part of the U.S. government that makes laws and is made up of the House of Representatives and the Senate. Members of Congress are chosen by the people of each state.

Constitution (kon-stih-TOO-shun)   The basic rules by which the United States is governed.

Constitutional Convention (kon-stih-TOO-shuh-nul kuhn-VEN-shun)   The political body that met in the summer of 1787 to create the U.S. Constitution.

currency (KUR-en-see)   Money.

democracy (di-MAH-kruh-see)   A government that is run by people who choose leaders and participate in making laws.

independence (in-dih-PEN-dents) Freedom from the control or support of other people; self-rule.

Magna Carta (MAG-na KAR-ta) The charter of English political and civil liberties granted by King John in 1215.

protest (PROH-test) An act of disagreement.

republic (ree-PUB-lik) A form of government in which the authority belongs to the people.

resolutions (reh-zuh-LOO-shunz) Official statements of the ideas of a group, voted on and put to use; a formal statement adopted by a group of people.

revenue (REH-veh-noo) Income.

tax (TACS) To make people pay money to support a government.

treaty (TREE-tee) An official agreement, signed and agreed upon by each party.

Web Sites

Due to the changing nature of Internet links, the Rosen Publishing Group, Inc., has developed an online list of Web sites related to the subject of this book. This site is updated regularly. Please use this link to access the list:

http://www.rosenlinks.com/tah/coco

Index

Credits

About the Authors: Sandra and Owen Giddens have written a number of books for Rosen Publishing. Sandra is a special education consultant and Owen is a psychotherapist. They have two teenage children, Justine and Kyle.

Photo credits:cover © Architect of the Capitol; p. 1 © Library of Congress, Rare Book and Special Collections Division; pp. 4, 14 (bottom) © Detroit Publishing Company Collection/Library of Congress Prints and Photographs Division; pp. 5, 17, 18, 24, 25, 26 © Bettmann/Corbis; pp. 6, 7, 8, 9, 10 © Hulton Archive/Getty Images; p. 11 © Corbis; pp. 12, 27 © General Records of the United States Government, Record Group 11/ National Archives and Records Administration; pp. 13 (top), 19 © Records of the Continental and Confederation Congresses and the Constitutional Convention, 1774-1789, Record Group 360/National Archives and Records Administration; p. 13 (bottom) © Library of Congress Geography and Map Division; pp. 14 (top), 21, 23 © Library of Congress Prints and Photographs Division; p. 15 © Farm Security Administration— Office of War Information Collection/Library of Congress Prints and Photographs Division; p. 16 © Historical Picture Archive/Corbis; p. 20 © 2003 Picture History LLC; p. 22 © Gerard W. Gawalt Manuscript Division/Library of Congress.

Designer: Geri Fletcher; Editor: Joann Jovinelly